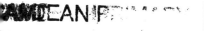

Contents

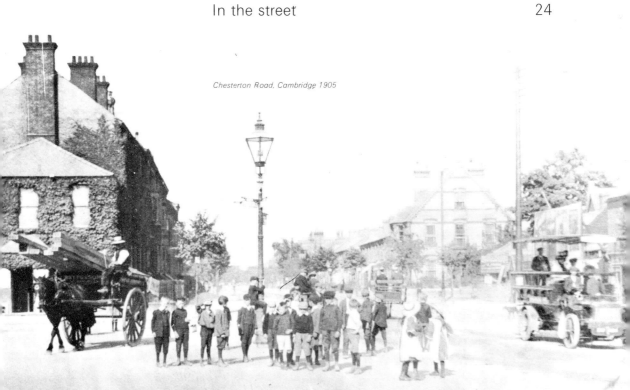

Chesterton Road, Cambridge 1905

Living
in the street

The children in
this old photograph
all lived in this
street. Some of their
mothers are in the
photograph, too.
Most of the people
are standing still,
smiling at the
camera.

They are posing for the photographer.

Can you see:

— the terraced cottages, or houses, each one joined to the
house next door
— the road made of sand and small stones
— a man and a boy on a horse and cart
— the street lights that were lit by gas.

Eleventh Street, Trafford Park, Manchester 1910

"Every evening the lamplighter came with a long pole to put the street lights on."

"It was a good neighbourhood, with rows of nice little cottages. If anyone was ill, or needed help, the whole street seemed to know."

Things to do

Start to make a book about the street 80 years ago. Call the first page *Houses in the street*.

Draw some houses like those in the picture. Include people standing outside the houses. Dress them like the people in the photograph.

Write about the people in the street in 1900. Think about where you live now. How is it different from the street in the photograph?

The street

**"A lot of streets didn't have anything at all on them.
We sometimes put cinders down to take up the mud."**

Cinders are pieces of burnt coal.
All the houses in the street had coal fires inside.
Look at the number of chimneys on the houses
in the old photographs.

**"Even the main roads were very rough.
They were made of flat setts, about the size
of a brick and just put down in the roadway."**

Milton Road, Cambridge 1905

Look carefully at this photograph. You can see flat setts in the road. Look at the number of chimneys on the houses, too.
The street also has one gas light.
Can you see the two lines running down the middle of the road? Electric trams went down this street. Their wheels ran on the lines and their engines used electricity from wires overhead.

Melbourne Street, Moston Lane, Manchester 1907

Things to do

Ask someone older than 70 about the street they lived in when they were your age.
— what was the street made of?
— what did it feel like to walk on?
In your book, write down what they tell you.

Ask someone who remembers the trams to tell you about them.

Traffic

"There was not as much traffic about as today. It was mostly horse-drawn, so it was much slower."

Chesterton Road, Cambridge 1905

In this old photograph you can see a delivery van pulled by a horse and an open-topped bus drawn by two horses.

Many trams were pulled by horses, too.

Today, many cars use this road. There are often traffic jams. There is a pedestrian crossing for you to use when you cross the road.

"I remember the one horse trams. We always used to save apples for the horse, because it stopped outside our door."

In this photograph look for:

— the tram driver. He needs his warm coat because he sits outside the tram.
— the conductor with his bag of tickets
— two passengers inside the tram
— the two men by the horse. They are the horsemen. Their job is to feed and care for the horses.
— the street tramway ticket. How much did it cost?

Things to do

Draw a street with some traffic in 1900. Remember that there were no cars, only horse-drawn vehicles.

Ask someone older than 70 what they remember about horses in the street where they lived.

Tradespeople

"We could get most things brought to our door, when I was a child. Bread came every day."

Look carefully at the picture.
— where was the photograph taken?
— what do you think was inside the van?
— how was the horse harnessed to the van?
— where are his reins?

When the driver sat in the van, he held the reins in his hands. When he pulled the left hand rein, the horse turned left. When he pulled the right hand rein, the horse turned right.

Another daily visitor to the street was the milkman.
In the photograph below, you can see the milkman
at the back of the cart pouring milk into a customer's can.
Walking behind him is a boy with a milk pram.
He pushed this up to people's front doors.

Levenshulme, Greater Manchester

Milk came in a huge
milk churn and was
measured out of this
into cans or jugs
at the door.

Things to do

How do you get your milk?
In your book, make two lists. Call one list *Milk delivery now.*
Write about your milkman today. Call the other list
Milk delivery then. Write about the milkmen in the photograph.

Draw pictures of tradespeople 80 years ago.

Coal

Coal was needed for the coal fire in the house. The coal fire was used to keep the house warm, to heat the water and to cook the food.

The coal cart below, which was pulled by a cart horse, is now in a museum. Look for:

— the wooden hames, or shafts, at the front of the cart. These were pulled down and the horse was harnessed between them.

— the scales and sacks. Some people bought a bag of special small coal, to get the fire started. It was called "best nuts".

"The coal place was in the cellar, underneath the house. Outside in the street, there was a manhole at the side of the wall. The coalman just tipped the coal out and we had to shovel it in. There was a chain inside the cellar to pull the cover closed."

Coalhole cover, Newmarket Road, Cambridge

Things to do

Ask someone old you know to tell you about when the coalman came.

Draw a picture of the whole family helping to shovel the coal into the cellar from the street outside.

Find out how much a bag of coal costs today. Where can you buy coal from?

The muffin man

Some traders walked down the street
selling things.
They were called hawkers.

**"I remember people
selling muffins
in the streets.
The muffins were
in a box covered
by a green cloth.
The man rang a bell
and people went
to their doors
with plates to put
the muffins on."**

Muffins were cakes with
fruit in them.
You ate them while they
were still warm.

This tray, bell and head pad belonged
to a muffin man. They are now in a museum.
Why do you think the muffin man
needed a head pad?

What do you think the muffin man
called out as he
came down the
street?

Things to do

Can you sing this song about the muffin man?
  "Can you see the muffin man,
    the muffin man, the muffin man?
  Can you see the muffin man,
    who lives in Drury Lane?"

Write the song down and draw a picture of the
muffin man. Put the picture in your book.

"Fresh fish!"

Mr. and Mrs. Binge, Huntingdon 1909

"They even used to come round every day with fresh fish.
She had a wicker basket on her arm full of fish.
There were winkles and shrimps on the barrow."

The street sellers in this photograph pushed a hand cart down the street. The cart was like a large wheelbarrow, but it had 2 wheels.

Look for:

— the 2 handles for pushing the cart
— the pint measure on top of the cart. They used to measure out the winkles and shrimps. (1 pint is about 0.5 litres.)
— the paper bags to wrap the fish in.

What do you think they called out as they walked down the street?

There were other street hawkers, too. Some sold cat's-meat, others sold firewood. One old lady remembers someone selling a sweet called Indian candy.

Things to do

Write about and draw pictures of some of the people who came down the street in 1900 selling things.

Think about where you live. Does anyone come into the street to sell things? How do they travel? What do they sell? What sounds do you hear that tell you they are there?

The corner shop

Most streets in 1900 had a corner shop. It was a friendly place, where people from the street often met each other and had a chat.

This shop belonged to the Kent family. Both Mr. and Mrs. Kent worked in the shop. What did they sell?

Stretford Road, Manchester 1906

"**The shop had a long counter with scales to weigh food. Tea, sugar and dried fruit were packed while we waited. The grocer took a square of paper and twisted it into a cone to make a paper bag.**"

16

This photograph was taken inside a shop.

Notice:

— the chair in front of the counter for the customer to sit on
— the advertising signs
— the large tins of biscuits, on the shelf
— the large tins of Bovril
— the barrels underneath the Bovril. There were large blocks of butter inside. The assistant patted the weight required.

Things to do

Look at the shop photographs. How many things were there in the shops then that we can still buy today?

Ask someone old you know if they have any stoneware jars, old tins, weights and scales.

Talk to someone who can tell you about shopping in a corner shop. What was different about shopping then from shopping in a supermarket today?

Street entertainers

Sometimes street entertainers came into the street.

**''The organ grinder often came down the street.
He had a barrel organ on wheels. He used to turn
a handle and we would dance to the music.''**

When the music stopped, the musician passed his hat
round and people put money in it.

**''Sometimes he had a monkey on top.
We loved to see the monkey and all the tricks he did.''**

Some organ grinders had a bird in a cage.

London 1905

St. John's Chapel, County Durham 1910

**"Once a man came round with a dancing bear.
Up and down he used to dance."**

The bear in the picture has a collar and lead,
like a dog. The trainer is holding the lead in his hand.

Things to do

In your book, write *Street entertainers*.
Pretend you are one of the children in the
photographs. Write about what you can see and
hear when either the organ grinder or the
dancing bear come into the street.

The motor car

"There were very few motor cars about then. Only the doctor had one."

Bolton, Greater Manchester 1905

Here is a photograph of a rich family
out in their new motor car.

Look for:

— the tyres. They were made of solid rubber.
— the lights which used paraffin oil
— the horn fixed to the steering wheel
— the boys with a rug round their legs.
There was no roof to the car and no luggage boot.
The car travelled at about 15 miles (24 km) an hour.

Things to do

Ask someone older than 70 about the first time
they saw a car.
What did it look like?
What did it sound like?

Look for a rally of old cars near where you live.

Collect pictures of old cars to put in your book.

Write about going for a ride in a car like
the one in the photograph.

Street games

"In the old days, when I was a child, we played hopscotch in the road and tops in the middle of the road."

The boys in the photograph are playing marbles in the middle of a road. It was safer to play in the street then, because there were very few cars about. Today children must go to a playground to play.

**"We played at buttons in the street.
You made a ring, stood away and threw
these buttons to get them in the ring.
Pearl buttons were worth a lot more
than the ordinary buttons."**

Sometimes children pushed
a hoop along with a stick;
sometimes they used
a whip to make a top spin.
Other children made up
their own games.

**"We played hoops a lot.
The hoops used to hang
on a hook outside the house."**

Things to do

Ask someone older than 70 about the games they played in the
street when they were young. Do you play any of the same games,
or games like them, with your friends?

Look for old toys in museums.

Try playing the game of buttons with your friends.

In the street

High Street, Linton, Cambridgeshire 1903

Today, many streets like the ones in this book are full of cars.
It is too dangerous to play in the street. Many corner shops have closed.
Would you have liked the street in 1900?

The following museums have things mentioned in this book
as part of their displays:

North of England Open Air Museum,
    Beamish Hall, Stanley, County Durham
The Yorkshire Museum of carriages and
    horse-drawn vehicles, York Mills,
    Aysgarth Falls, North Yorkshire
National Motor Museum, Palace House,
    Beaulieu, Hampshire
Transport Museum, Newtownards Road,
    Belfast, Northern Ireland

Transport Museum, Bearland, Gloucester
Transport and Archaeology Museum,
    36 Hight Street, Hull, East Yorkshire
Science Museum, Exhibition Road,
    South Kensington, London
The Shuttleworth Collection,
    Old Warden Aerodrome, Bedfordshire
Cambridge and County Folk Museum,
    Castle Street, Cambridge.

Children and history

These books aim to introduce children to history by using as a starting point, places and people familiar to them.

This book was compiled from information collected by children talking to old people they knew. The photographs were added later. Oral history can be used in three ways:
a) you can play children a tape recording you have made
b) you can invite someone elderly to answer the children's questions
c) the children can collect their own information using either a tape recorder or a written questionnaire.
In this last way, children can resource their own project.

It will be necessary to prune and transcribe the interview material, to extract information which is relevant to the project. Sometimes the adult does this; sometimes the children. Try to resist the temptation of "tidying up" or "improving" the grammar in an oral interview and let the past speak for itself. History for the children will then become a living thing, not simply something that comes packaged in books.

There are many projects that lend themselves to oral history:
— the daily routine of the past at home and at work
— local occupations and crafts that may have died out
— exceptional events in the history of the neighbourhood or nation such as wars, disasters and celebrations.
Old photographs, tools, streets and buildings can come alive for children when someone talks about them; and topics like childhood, the family and the community can be given a personal dimension.

Once the children have made contact with the people who made history, it should be easy to borrow photographs and objects from them for a display. In addition, many local museums, listed in the annual publication *Museums and Galleries in Great Britain and Ireland* (ABC Publications, Oldhill, London Road, Dunstable, Bedfordshire), have exhibits and pictures from the recent past. Some local libraries and Record Offices have collections of old photographs and will supply copies on request, where possible.

Acknowledgements

We are grateful to the following for permission to reproduce photographs:
BBC Hulton Picture Library, page 18; Cambridge and County Folk Museum, page 12; Cambridgeshire Collection, pages 1, 4, 6 and 24; Cambridgeshire Record Office, Huntingdon, pages 14–5 and front cover; Greenwich Local History Library, back cover; Kodak Museum, inside front cover and page 22; Manchester Studies Unit, pages 2–3, 5, 8, 9 left, 16, 20–1 and 23; North of England Open Air Museum, Beamish, pages 17 and 19; Science Museum, London, Crown ©, page 10.
Photographs on pages 7, 9 right, 11 and 13 are by Gwil Owen.

LONGMAN GROUP UK LIMITED
Longman House,
Burnt Mill, Harlow, Essex CM20 2JE, England
and Associated Companies throughout the world

First published 1981
Eighth impresson 1992
ISBN 0 582 18435 5

The publisher's policy is to use paper manufactured from sustainable forests.

Produced by Longman Singapore Publishers Pte Ltd
Printed in Singapore

Into the past

edited by **Sallie Purkis**

Longman

3. At school in 1900

Sallie Purkis

Longman

To the reader

This book will help you to go back in time: from the present into the past. When you have read a page, you will find some "Things to do". You can make a book of your own about school in 1900.

Talk to someone who is older than 70. They may be able to tell you what school was like then. Have a list of questions you want to ask them. Collect the answers on a tape recorder or in writing. Tell your friends what you find out.

Try to borrow some old things about school from your grandparents or other elderly friends you know. You can have an exhibition. Here are some things to do with schools which you may be able to collect: slates, dip-in pens, photographs, books, prizes, reports, medals, certificates, concert programmes.

Ask your Headteacher how old your school is. All schools have a special diary called a Log Book. You may be able to write a history of your school.

Some museums display old school things. See if there is one near where you live.

All sentences in **"bold type"** in this book are the things old people remember about their school days. The words are exactly what they said.

Photographers in 1900 looked like this. You had to stand still while the photograph was taken.